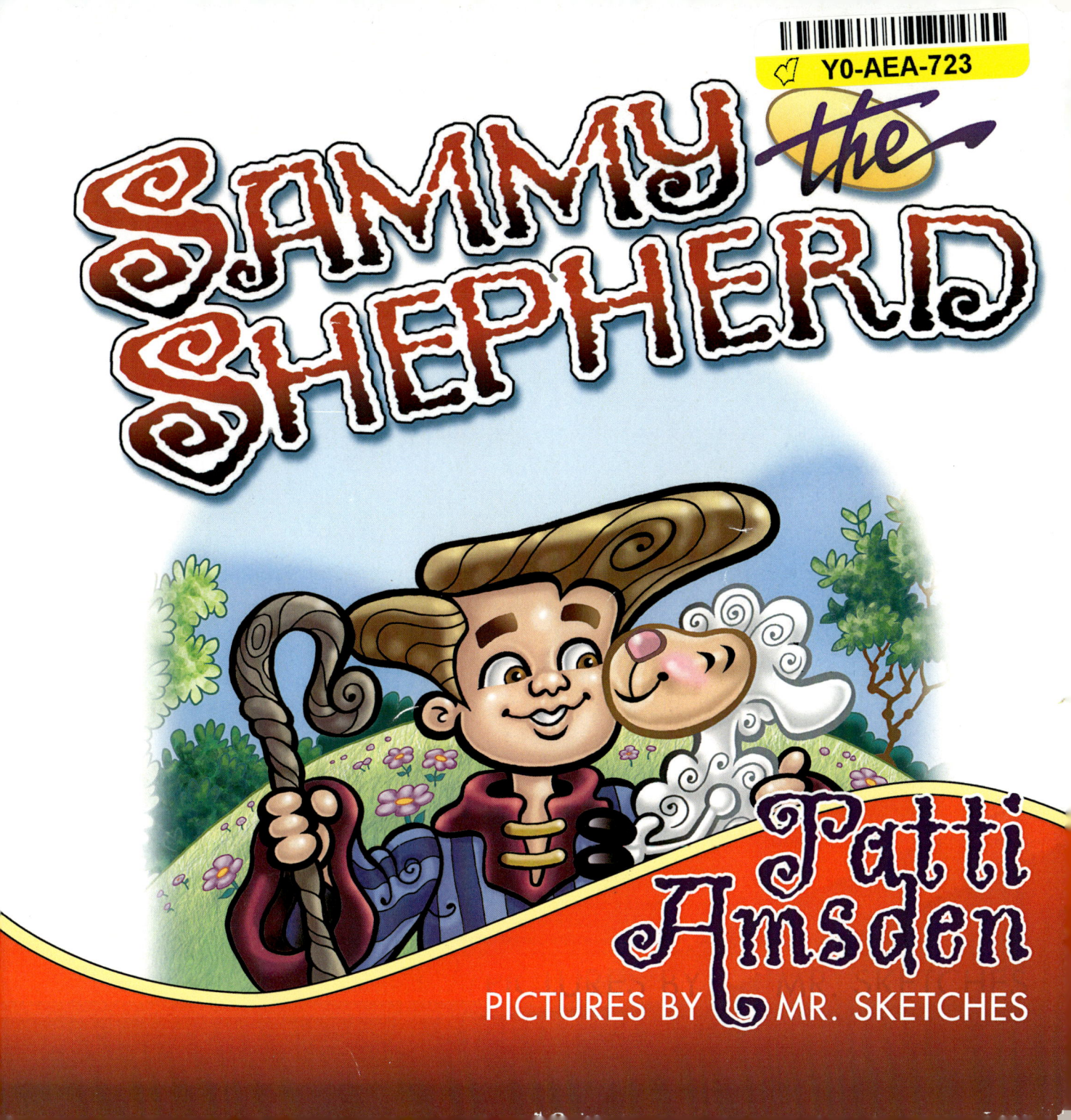

Sammy the Shepherd

Patti Amsden

PICTURES BY MR. SKETCHES

SAMMY THE SHEPHERD by Patti Amsden
Copyright ©2014 by Patti Amsden
Printed in the USA

All rights reserved. This book is protected under the copyright laws of the United States of America. This book may not be copied or reprinted for commercial gain or profit. Reproduction of text, cover, and illustrations in whole or in part without the express written consent of the author or publisher is not permitted.

ISBN 978-0-9862027-0-4
For worldwide distribution

This Book Belongs To:
_____

A Gift From:
_____

Date: _____

4

The story – they tell us – happened so far away
That no one knows for sure all the details today.

But now – stretch your minds – imagine tonight,
And maybe, just maybe – we'll get it near right.

A long time ago and far, far from here,
Shepherds rested in fields with their flocks lying near.

That night – it was just like all nights before.
In fact, Sam the Shepherd thought that sheep were a bore!

They bah and they bleat and feed on the hill.
Sam knew, for the shepherd, there was seldom a thrill.

An occasional lion
 would threaten the flock.
Shepherd Sammy liked those nights;
 he liked them a lot.

He'd take out his staff;
 he'd rumble and roar.
He'd show that old lion
 what a shepherd was for!

What tales he would spin
 of the foe and the fight
'Til young boys would say,
 "Shepherd Sam, he's all right."

7

8

That night held a little chill in the air,
But no beast of prey and no cause of care.

Sam the Shepherd was thinking of a game he could play,
So the night would pass quickly and turn into day.

Whoever would think — Whoever did know
That the night sky would light up and glory would show?

But that's just what happened. Sam looked up and there
A bright star from heaven had begun to appear.

He lifted his staff. He was ready to fight.
Then somehow he knew he could trust that bright light.

He watched as the light beams
    fell to the ground,
'Til his gaze was disrupted
    by a loud, booming sound —

From the voice of a being
    so glistening bright;
Sam knew it was an angel —
    an angel all right.

"Good tidings and great joy,"
    the angel did say,
"Good tidings to all men
    I bring you this day!"

"This day there is born
    the Savior of all;
He's wrapped and he's lying
    in a manger — a stall."

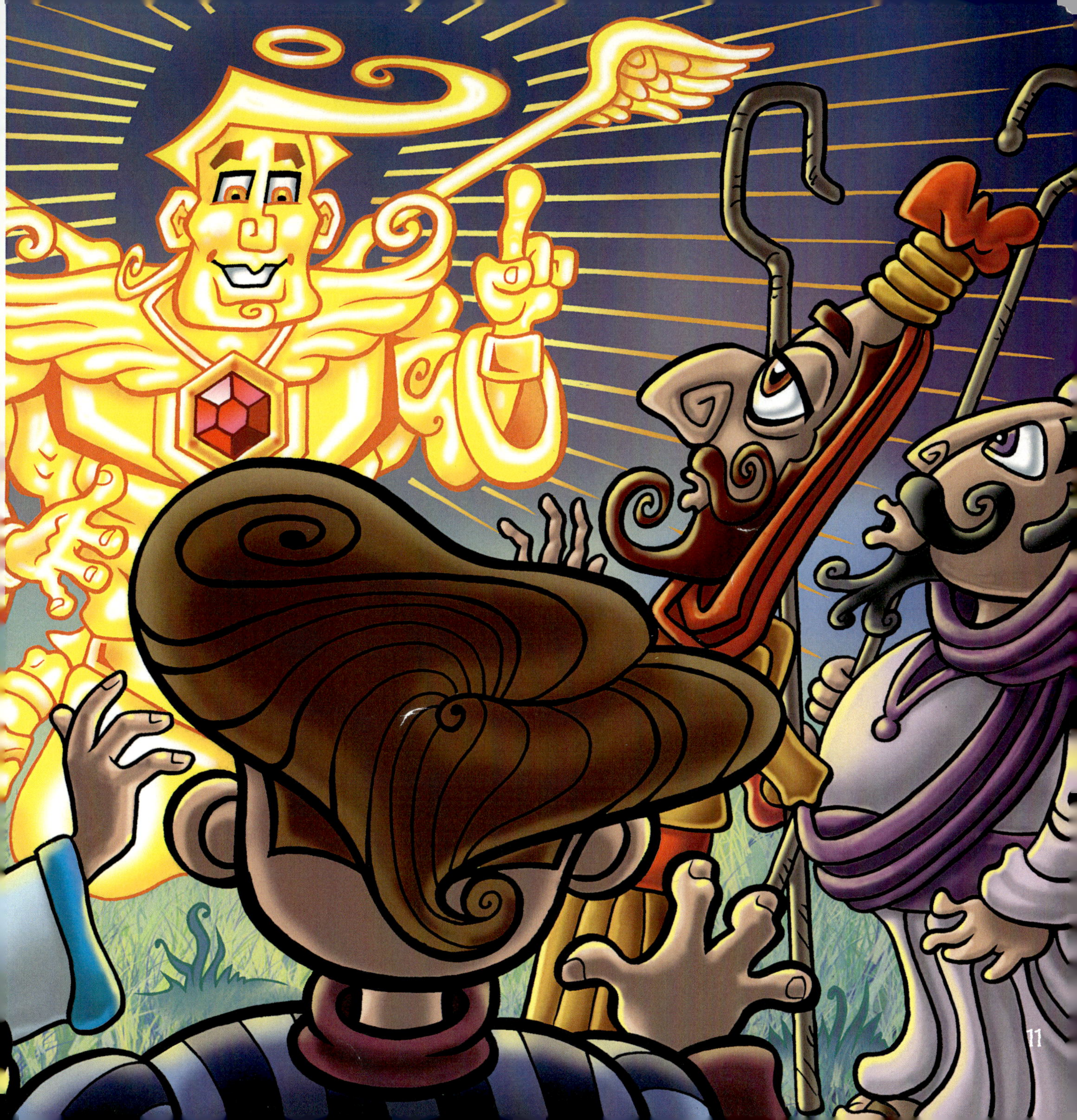

Before Shepherd Sam could utter a word,
Songs of praises from angels began to be heard.

And a great host appeared in the heaven on high
As the angelic choir filled up the night sky.

14

And then it was over – the night quiet, serene.
Sam pondered on just what he'd heard and he'd seen.

He decided he must go, in haste find the one
Whom angels had worshipped and called him God's Son.

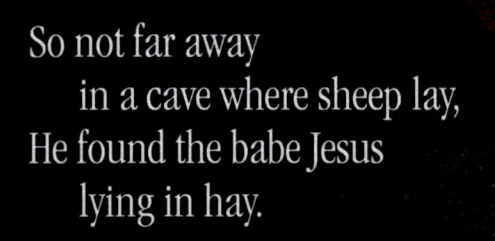

So not far away
  in a cave where sheep lay,
He found the babe Jesus
  lying in hay.

No grand palace there
  nor a great kingly bed
Was the resting place
  for this baby's head.

Shepherd Sam thought it strange
  that this One highly praised
Would be laid in a stall
  where the animals grazed.

17

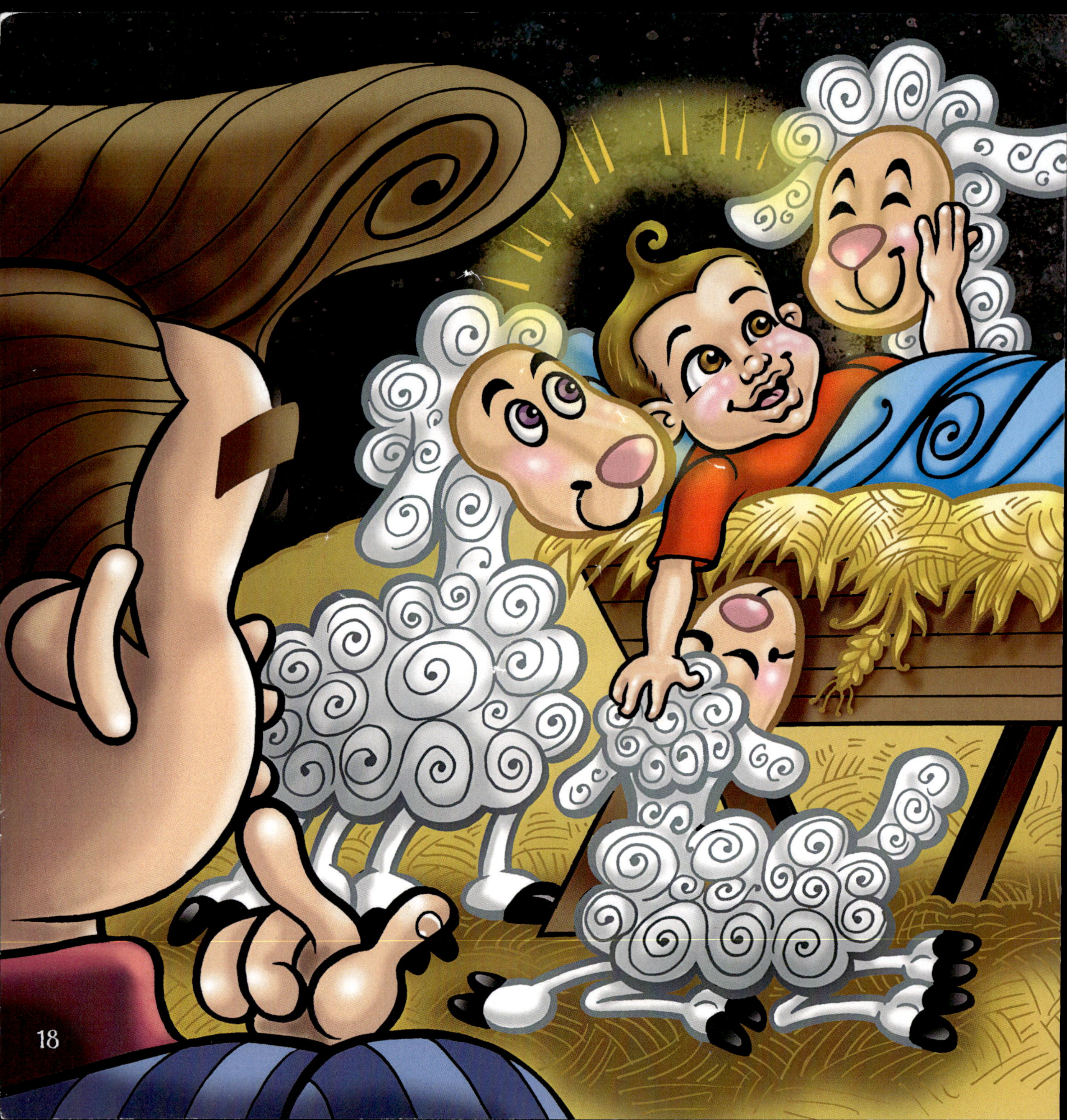

Then the thought dawned upon
    Sam the Shepherd that night,
"This manger might fit
    the babe's calling just right."

"Perhaps He shall be
    a shepherd as I,
And tend to a flock
    and answer the cry –

Of those gone astray,
    those lost from the fold,
He'd retrieve and rescue
    from the dark and the cold."

Shepherd Sam smiled within
    as he thought of the day
When Jesus would shepherd
    His flock in the Way.

And sure – if a lion would threaten His flock,
Shepherd Jesus would fight him. He'd fight him – why not?

He'd take out his staff; He'd rumble and roar;
He'd show that old lion what a shepherd is for.

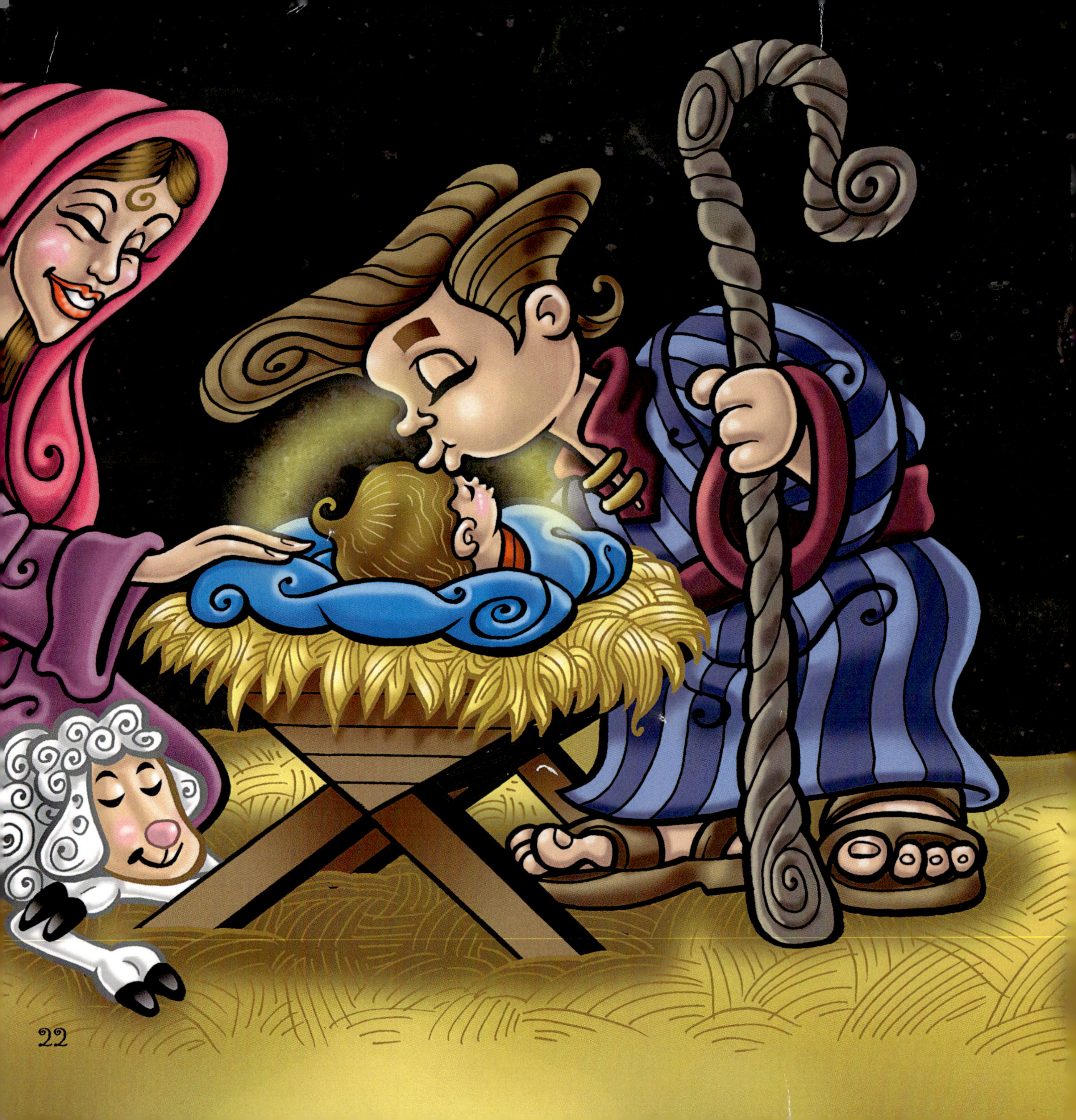

Sam stayed by the babe for the rest of the night
Then returned to his flock at the dawn's early light.

As soon as he could, Shepherd Sam went to town
To find all the young boys who oft gathered round.

They eagerly awaited the tale of his fight.
What predator strong had he vanquished that night?

25

Sam told of the angels, the song, and the star,
The babe in the manger — God's Son from afar.

27

"Wow!" said the young boys,
 "The Savior has come.
Shepherd Sam has now seen Him.
 Sam is the one –

Whom heaven has chosen
 to reveal this joy,
To tell the great story
 of God's Shepherd Boy."

"This life as a shepherd
 is great," Sam proclaimed.
"It's better than wealth,
 or fortune, or fame."

We are told that Sam learned a great lesson that night –
That shepherding's more than an occasional fight.

A shepherd is born from the Father above.
A shepherd has God's heart – a heart filled with love.

A shepherd will care for the strong and the weak,
Will feed sheep, will lead sheep, and continually seek –

Still waters, green pastures where the flock can be fed,
And places of safety where they can be bed.

For the Lord Baby Jesus came down to the earth
To rescue lost people and offer new birth.

He left an example. He gave us the call
Of loving our neighbor, giving service to all.

Shepherd Sam learned the lesson that we all should know –
When we shepherd like Jesus, His flock – it will grow.

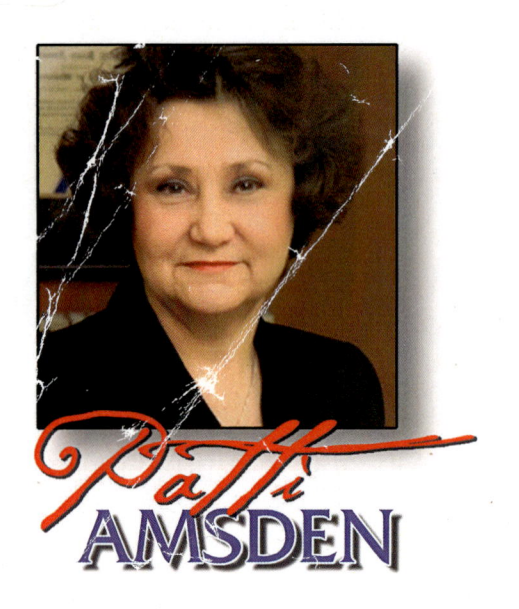

About The Author

Dr. Patti Amsden is an author and Bible scholar. In addition to serving as an associate pastor and itinerate minister, she has also invested many years teaching the Bible to students in a Christian academy. Having written a number of theological books and high school Bible curricula, Dr. Amsden now applies her skills to children's books in this entertaining and inspirational trilogy, which looks at the nativity event through the eyes of a shepherd lad, a young magi boy, and a little angel.

About The Illustrator

David Wilson is also known by some children as Mr. Sketches, a title that was created for a children's TV show that broadcast nationally on TBN for about 3 years. The pen name has stuck for over 20 years in various aspects of his art career, such as children's books, caricatures, and The Power Team comic books, to name a few. At the age of 5, he was born again and fear of the dark was dispelled when an angel appeared and said, "Fear not!" From that early experience, children have been a major focus for the sketches of art, which flow from his heart.